Wordsong

Robin Skelton

Wordsong

TWELVE BALLADS

1983
Sono Nis Press
Victoria, British Columbia
Canada

Copyright © 1983 by Robin Skelton

Canadian Cataloguing in Publication Data

Skelton, Robin, 1925-
    Wordsong

Poems.
ISBN 0-919203-42-6

I. Title.
PS8537.K44W67   C811'.54   C83-091113-8
PR9199.3.S537W67

This book has been financially assisted by
the Canada Council Block Grant Program and the
Government of British Columbia through
the British Columbia Cultural Fund and
British Columbia Lottery Revenues.

Published by
SONO NIS PRESS
1745 Blanshard Street
Victoria, British Columbia V8W 2J8

Designed and printed in Canada by
MORRISS PRINTING COMPANY LTD.
Victoria, British Columbia

for
SEAN
who
listens

Contents

Preface

In 1981, when my *Collected Shorter Poems* appeared from the Sono Nis Press, I turned my mind to the much more difficult problem of putting together a *Collected Longer Poems* and discovered almost immediately that there was a maverick in the herd. The sequence of ballads, all but one written in the late fifties, simply did not belong with the more meditative long poems and sequences such as *The Dark Window, Timelight, Callsigns,* and *Landmarks.* They were far more rhetorical, frequently rumbustious, and sometimes bawdy, and the voice in which they spoke was a different voice altogether. Moreover, inasmuch as they presented anything of a consistent viewpoint, this viewpoint did not only differ from but was largely at odds with that of the other poems. Nevertheless, I could not find it in me to abandon them to the near-oblivion into which they had been forced by the passage of years. Moreover, even though they did form a kind of progress, moving from the ballad as a story to something quite other, the sequence as a whole had never been put together in a book. All save the two Ballads of the Muse and the *Ballad of Billy Barker* appeared in my collection of 1960, *Begging the Dialect,* which has long been unavailable to all but assiduous searchers in second-hand bookshops. The two Ballads of the Muse were thrown out of that collection by my editor at Oxford University Press, who thought them too bawdy for publication by his respectable firm. These were published separately in a limited edition printed by the Rampant Lions Press in Cambridge, England in 1960 and reappeared in my *Selected Poems* of 1968 published by McClelland & Stewart, which also contained the *Ballad of Billy Barker* that had been added to the sequence in 1965 and published that year as a pamphlet by the Morriss Printing Company Ltd. of Victoria. These later books have also been out of print for some years.

Six of the twelve ballads are either set in the landscape of the West Penwith area of Cornwall, England, or derive their imagery from it. The exceptions are the *Ballad of Billy Barker* (though Barker was a Cornishman), the Ballads of *Need*, of *The Watcher*, and of *Birth* (which could be set in Cornwall as well as anywhere), and the two *Ballads of the Muse*. All, however, appear to me to be dealing with similar subject matter and speaking in similar voices, so that the series does have an overall cohesiveness.

In putting this small collection together I have found it necessary to make some revisions to the original text, but I do not think that, in doing so, I have betrayed the original vision. I hope, indeed, that I have clarified it, even though it is not a vision that now, so many years later, I am able wholly to share.

ROBIN SKELTON

Victoria, B.C.
December 1982

A FIRST BALLAD OF THE MUSE

You, the listener, listen.
I stand where words begin
and time is called. Come over to
the snug I'm harboured in.
My nails of heels tack down the black
and glisten of the street,
and I'm the one original whore
that sweats the winding sheet.

I call you quietly and slow.
Time is a strange strange thing.
You spin a history out and find
the history begin.
You flip a penny memory and
go in at your own door,
and there a new conclusion lies
and stares up from the floor.

Come over here and name your want.
The blowfly crawls the wall.
Names are the only lonely watchers
when your apples fall,
and we'll be one name in the dark,
as in the dark love lies
flat up against the window catch
that rattles at the skies.

We'll spell one word this cocksure night.
You'll have your sentence fling
its small-shot at my belly's shout
the drill hall we'll be in;
I'll have you sentry quick as wink
and grip your gun like rock;
I wear my breasts as armament
and fight each night I look.

I put your word into my mouth
and spell your sentence bare.
A bright bone button winks at you
up from the bedroom floor.
The creased cloth grins. The hot sheet shifts.
We meet in one wide bed.
The blowfly crawls the knocking wall
and the great word is said.

It's shouted out. Come closer, dear.
I know my voice is raw
as any waiting twice-timed bitch
that has you in her door,
but o that husky edge you hear
is what the women cry
who ply short-time in the arcade
and know the hearse go by.

For time is short. I talk about
what every man jack's found,
locked in the threadbare winding sheet
with woman and with wound.
But I'm not hiring minutes out.
You have the need I am.
We meet in one where the knife hangs up
above the tangled ram.

We meet in one. One is our name.
The blowfly crawls the wall.
But names knit where that Madame smiles
her knife blade on us all;
though I'll drive deep your bargain
and not a penny's found,
we beat upon the black full point
that blocks us in the end.

Bed down with me and you'll not get
your lonely name again.
My tongue will talk your muscle down
and my throat speak your pain.
My hand will cramp your sentence out,
my thighs dream in your bed,
and my black nails of heels tack down
the pavestones of your dead.

Give me your look. That eye you have
will find the deep of me,
but look me back into the eye
and I'll own all you see.
I'll walk my pitch and clack my heels
and fumble buttons back
from all the generations that
would have you on your rack.

Step over here. I am your Fate —
you're fated to a whore,
and there's no scented night-dress hanging
up behind my door,
no midnight pool or pink champagne,
but what's beneath my skirt
is common knowledge, and I am
as common as the dirt.

Common is the word I am,
and I am that to all.
Step over here and take your chance
to have your apples fall.
Stake your luck deep and it will turn
within the tossing bed;
the blowfly walks the knocking wall
till the last word is said.

The blowfly crawls the brothel wall.
The clock winks like a pin.
The shortest time is long enough
to get your one word in.
The shortest time is double-backed
to let the sentence spend
until we come upon the black
that blocks us in the end.

The black full point. I am. You are.
A syntax shakes the house.
Words are what lean us up against
the separating glass.
My nails of heels tap gravestones down
until the gravestones call.
I am the word man had at first
and shall have when I fall.

A BALLAD OF BILLY BARKER

A gay young widow woman
with eyes as green as glass,
and a bandy-legged prospector
with slum upon his ass;
you split your sides to think of it,
but I lie stiff as stone:
it's curtains now for English Bill
in Victoria Old Men's Home.

On Williams Creek in August
back in sixty-two
the claims ran dry. The black sand let
no speck of colour through.
Ned Stout came down the canyon
and found his gulch and struck;
I followed him, staked out my claim,
and drove down through the rock.

Jumped ship, I did, and followed up
the blinding yellow dream.
The Fraser lashed its rolling stones
till mud was silver cream;
the walls of Hell's Gate cliffed me in
and Jackass Mountain shook
its dirt-brown back in mockery as
I trailed to stake my luck.

Seven of us worked that shaft.
The sun danced with the heat.
Ten feet we went and nothing showed.
Ten feet and then ten feet.
At thirty feet the cloud came up;
the sky was solid lead;
the windlass juddered at each hoist;
the wind sobbed for the dead.

Seven of us choked for breath.
I went down in the pit.
At forty feet the rain came down;
we took another foot.
A crazy sailor and six men
hauled rope till they were blind;
at fifty feet no colours showed
and even hope was mined.

Hope, Faith, Prayer were all mined out
and rubble piled up high
around the shaft-house hacked out from
the pines that hacked the sky;
mud welled; rain swaled; ropes cut and slid,
and heart and mouth were dry.

At sea the waters curve away
green satin from the bow,
and foam as thick as milk swirls out
along the track we plough,
and waves heave tall as hills and fall
like hills upon the deck.
The hills that stood round Williams Creek
would neither bend nor break.

The hills that frowned their forest black
above our hunch and sweat
rocked no horizons for our eyes,
nor shone out in the night
with greens and blues and grains of gold
as I've seen on the sea.
We took another foot. The dream
stood shuddering over me;

the yellow dream, the blinding dream
I'd taken for my life
stood over me. I felt its breath.
Its eyes cut like a knife.
I took another foot. Time stopped.
I heard it end my life.

I heard it finish, and I struck.
Five dollars to the pan;
and seven men on Williams Creek
went crazy to a man.
A thousand dollars every foot
we took out from that clay
and seven men on Williams Creek
were blinded by the day.

Drinks we had. Three days we drank
and all on English Bill.
I think I drank a thousand lives
at every swig and spill,
a thousand miners trailing north,
a thousand narrow pits
upon the benches by the creeks
where golden bones would sit.

I think in every glass I saw
a face and then a face;
a woman with long yellow hair
leaned into my embrace,
a widow with eyes green as grass
and lips as red as blood,
but at her back another face
as black as the wet wood,

another face as black as wood,
with skin as soft as slum
and eyes as blind as pebbled quartz,
and gaping mouth as dumb
as Blessing's mouth, or Barry's mouth
that opened as he swung.

I met her in Victoria by
the bitter chilling strait.
Some traded skins. I traded gold
and traded for a mate,
a London widow woman
and her golden hair and luck:
I took her up the Fraser
through the roaring mocking rock.

I took her up to Barkerville;
I should have let her be.
The gold ran out; the claim ran dry;
she ran loose as the sea;
her greens of satin, foams of silk
heaved up to prow on prow:
the sea's a wicked smother, but
I know a worse one now.

The sea's a wicked country;
its green hills lift and drown:
but earth's a played-out working
when you've thrown your money down.
I worked as cook; I begged; I washed;
my pans were grey with stone:
it's curtains now for English Bill
in Victoria Old Men's Home.

It's headstones now for English Bill.
My drinking roaring mouth
burns cancer where her kisses burned
and has a graver drouth,
and as I gape I see her face,
but then that other face
that looked on me in Williams Creek
and rotted like the race —

the race of men that dragged their packs
up canyons to the creek,
the race that heard my pick crack down
into that yellow strike,
whose deaths built law and church and state
upon my broken stone,
but Billy Barker's dead and gone
in Victoria Old Men's Home.

A BALLAD OF A DEATH

Admiral Sir Cloudesley Shovell, on his way back from the Mediterranean in 1707, hanged a man on board ship. Before the man died he prophesied that wherever Sir Cloudesley was buried no green thing would grow. On 22 October 1707 Sir Cloudesley's ship, *The Association,* was wrecked in the Scillies on the Clerk and Bishop Rocks, and he was washed up in Porthellick Cove. There, early the next morning, a woman found him, and killed him for the emerald ring upon his hand. She confessed to the murder upon her death-bed thirty years later.

For Gladys and Albert Curnow

Let propriety go hang.
I've had a drink or two.
And all the swimming fish are shoaled
to white and wander through
the three spars of my evening mind
stuck on the seas' bed,
and the great nets drag their shawls
over my figurehead.

A quarter of a century
walks like the one dark night.
Down on the Clerk and Bishop Rocks
you'll see her timbers float
from when she split that night that is
the last night of each day
I clamp the ring upon the glass
and look out on the sea.

I rehearse this lamp night
what I'll tell when I die.
The great blind crowder of the sea
winks with a wrecker's eye.
Knock it back and have one with
the ring upon my hand;
I found it in Porthellick Cove,
the finger scrabbling sand.

His arms flung out like on a cross,
drowned as the dead he lay,
mouth bubbling like a broken crab.
What else is there to say?
He was dead, or good as dead,
on his right hand a ring.
My hand that had no ring at all
heard the blind crowder sing.

I've watched the red hair swoop my skin
in mirrors cracked as stone
a quarter of a century,
and the thin finger bone
blaze green, crooking at my ear
to push the red tide back,
and the mouth smile stiff to find
a man's mouth kiss and suck.

Who gives a damn? The hair's my own
and red as then it was.
My skin's as white, they tell me,
and the ring green as grass —
green as the hollow of the seas
when a white comber curls
out of the black waters' hill
in the scream of gulls.

It was a great man died there.
A wisdom took my hand
the day he lay wrenched as a root
and scrabbled the wide sand.
If you take a great man off
you put a greatness on.
What if I helped him under
at the blind crowder's song?

Let the moral sniffwits stare.
I'll tell it when I die.
From that I got this way of talk
and this dark in my eye
that every last night swims the white
spars on the seas' bed,
and knows the great nets drag their shawls
over a figurehead.

How the hell time turns me back
on the backtiding sea
until I watch him walk the deck
is what possesses me.
He hanged a man from his masthead
while the ship ran slow.
"Wherever you are coffined down
no green thing shall grow. . . . "
Strapped like an anchor in his chain,
the darkness in his eye,
"Wherever you shall batten down
there's no green for the sky."

Sir Cloudesley Shovell hanged that man.
He strapped him on a cloud
that swung the masts through time and time
until fulfilment roared
the Bishop and the Clerk up through
the bottom timbers, and
one green thing quivered where he lay,
and all the rest was sand.

Let your fingers to the glass;
the weather needs it black.
For all the name he had then
from Barbary and the Rock,
the green thing left him by my hand,
(I'll tell it when I die),
and in Porthellick Cove they found
no green to give the lie.

Fulfilment is the name they give.
I've had a drink or two.
A quarter of a century
lies between we two.
And many a man has lain between
but still the fishes thread
the cross spars in the green of deep
that holds the figurehead.

Admiral Sir Cloudesley Shovell.
The clouds were running thin
the day they slapped a spade on top
the box they put him in,
thin as a skein of carder's wool
and strung out like a drift
to snare the mewing gulls and drag
wild weather from the west.

No grass grows there. No green at all.
I walk Porthellick sand.
Men always have a question
of the ring upon my hand.
Men always have their answer,
and shall have till I'm dead
and the great nets drag their shawls
over my figurehead.

A BALLAD OF A MINE

The Wheal Owles mining disaster occurred in the early years of this century when the miners broke through into an adjacent flooded mine called Come Lucky. Nineteen men and a boy were drowned, and the sole survivor from the working where the accident took place walked the roads of West Penwith as a pedlar for the remainder of his life. The shoring up of the workings with pit props is known in Cornwall as "keeping the country abroad." At a museum in Zennor there is a miner's lamp inscribed with the words "Goodbye the day. Good luck to me."

Between Botallack and the light
I took the lamp below,
the tunnelled summers of the mind
black and sour as sloe.
The daybreak brought the darkness down;
at day's end night was free
to dowse the lamp that carried down
"Goodbye the day. Good luck to me."

You have to go a long way round
to have a history told.
For twenty years I've seen the lifted
white head of the road
that hills it up Nancherrow side
frown grey as a carn
and held my tongue against its spate
to keep disaster warm.

Nineteen paces to the gate
and then a half pace more
I count the steps in those men's names
who faced the waters' roar.
Nineteen years and a bit.
(The bit was but a lad.)
Time goes a long way round about
to get a learned thing said.

Wheal Owles above the burning sea
that dazzles out the eye
of any man who knows the night
mine down into the day,
we bent to break the clagged ore out
while breath was harsh as scree
and sweat slid down the muscled back.
Goodbye the day. Good luck to me.

I've never had a dream of what
the first great morning said
when the bag of water broke
for man to breach his head,
or when my father first set down
my name within his mind,
and swung his lamp down at the door
warped with the wet sea wind.

I've never had a word come in
the hollow of the dark
to tell the first great watcher's word
who broke life from the rock,
though then it was a thing enough
and all the folk stood round
as they stood at Wheal Owles the day
I got the chapter learned.

Learned me the chapter, that day did.
Nineteen paces more.
Nineteen paces and a bit
from this door to that door.
What I have here I have to sell.
With breath as harsh as scree
we bent to break the black ore out.
Goodbye the day. Good luck to me.

We kept the country well abroad.
The road was clear as gin.
There was no crack or rotten tack
the working we were in.
Come Lucky nudged us on one side
but that was flooded out,
a house of water, and a house
we asked no visit at.

Come Lucky. But we have our luck.
Nineteen and a bit
your garden hedges by the road;
I've learned the length of it
from tread and tread for half a life,
the half of life let free
from mornings carrying down the shift
"Goodbye the day. Good luck to me."

Goodbye the day. Come Lucky lay
and nudged us in the pit.
A dead man took the steel drill up
and had his luck of it.
A pinhole. But a prick, a pin.
The crack starred out like light,
light water-black. The wall of black
clapped like a Canaanite,

ran like a river down the latch
and sneck of deadman's door,
broke like a bag of thunderclap
upon the carn-cragged moor;
alive and kicking, wombed with flood,
nineteen and a lad
spun round, spun round, the long way round
to say their history dead.

The country was well kept abroad.
I ran through waters' house.
The great wave, shouldered like a moor,
tore all heaven loose,
and at the crack of night came luck.
The black wet let me be.
The ladder held into the shaft.
Goodbye the day. Good luck to me.

The ladder held into the shaft
and this head met the sky.
Nineteen years and a bit
I've walked that history dry.
Nineteen men and but a lad.
Did darkness break that one might see?
I learned the chapter off by heart.
Goodbye the day. Good luck to me.

A BALLAD OF THE KNOCKING STONES

Kenidjack Carn dominates the moor above Tregeseal, and miners from Botallack had to cross the moor on their way home if they lived on the other side of the peninsula. There are many stone circles and Bronze and Iron Age villages hereabouts, and the moors are notoriously haunted.

For Tony Connor

I talk the way I only am.
Dust rises on the floor.
There is a whisper rattles at
the sneck outside the door.
Time clacks the latch to let time in
and mists lift off the sea
and old wives' words lie near the bone
when all the winds are free.

Trees whipped like briars across the rain
that drove down all its drills
upon the road, and bracken
like bladderwrack lay spilled
on pocked stones shoved up from the tide
and sweep of the long moor.
From pit to bed is a long tread,
and stones stand at the door.

Not that I make a tale of it.
The common words come out
with callouses upon their hands
to turn the stones about.
The stones turn in each breath I pull
till I am gravestone flat,
and every bed-dark that night walk
is what I'm sleeping at.

Sixty Level is two miles run
under the knocking sea.
The boulders roll on the black sea bed.
You hear them as you knee
the rockside or the iron rung
or walk the workings back
into night on Kenidjack moor,
the bracken like bladderwrack.

You'll hear the same things over.
The words walk in my head;
echo and back, and echo back
the road knocked at my tread,
and in my head the boulders rolled
and boulders humped the moor.
From pit to bed is a long tread,
and stones stand at the door.

God's Acre spreads its deadman stones
a bone's throw from the shore,
but below the Carn the stones
laid out upon the moor
hump warted granite shoulders up
and crawl the furze like toads.
The boulders knocked inside my head
along that night-walk road.

I crossed the moor from pit to bed.
From pit to bed I'd known
across the moor no body lift
its shadow but my own,
but this night-walk the loud and black
of rain drove with a will
till under the shoulder of the Carn
the everywhere fell still.

The big moon shoved its brightness up,
the Carn shone wet as lead,
and acred shadows dragged their nets
upon the moor's sea bed
as by me there a stone stood up,
rose up without a sound,
while out by Tregeseal I saw
the circle change its ground.

What can be made to mark that stone
and give the telling word?
The language alters like the moor
with the grave's truth unheard.
The meanings lock their meanings in;
though men must mean to say,
you'll get no answer of the door
that swings the light away.

Words drop into their sockets like
the stone poles of the door,
and lock a meaning out or in
to keep the wall secure.
And mining deep you hear the stones
turn on the deep sea bed,
and language alters like a tide
under their coverlid.

Language alters like the tide.
I tell no tale at all.
But every bed-night I have known
I hear those boulders roll.
I saw stones dance like they were men.
It was the earth unlocked,
and men like stones, or stones of men
danced till the country shook.

The moor stirred like a great sea bed
where salt webs shift and fold,
and language comes a long way round
to get their dancing told,
but words add wind to meaning
and the meaning's in the head
that hears the knocking boulders talk
tall on the black sea bed.

The meaning puts the fury out,
and round about I go
as those white stones went round about
to tell the thing I know.
I talk the way the boulders talked
the dance out on the moor.
From pit to bed is a long tread,
and stones stand at the door.

From pit to bed is a long tread.
I knocked on my own door.
The stones had stopped the stillness that
had covered me before.
The stones had stopped the stillness,
and I heard the knocking sea,
the dance of stone, the dance of bone,
and all the dead were free.

A BALLAD OF THE FOUR FISHERS

For Michael and Margaret Snow

I got four sons across my bed
below the harbour wall,
and April slid like silver eels
when I was marrying tall;
though bells and bells and bells rocked out
above the piled-up town
four sons jumped in my star-splayed loin
and all my wounds were drowned.

"Turn to time's other side," he said;
"You'll have your net-mesh swag
with heavier leaping fish than any
unblessed nets could drag;
you'll haul it full." Nine months I hauled;
the bag of waters broke:
whose was the voice I recognized
when my own belly spoke?

I got four sons. They gave me all
that flesh and blood could bear.
The holy dust ran like a mouse
below the churching door.
Sands scuttled fast as winds blew up
before He blessed each head;
the name-words tasted in my mouth
of the red salt of blood.

If you've seen stars out on a night
the rocked boats' moorings twitch,
gulls idling white upon the black,
or, troubled with time's itch,
walked corkscrew streets on to the top
to stare down on the town
and watched the one by one lamps snuff
the one by one blinds down;

if you've walked back from tides to find
the wet slap of the fish
flipping its flat white belly on
the friday of the dish,
the lifted hands clasped cockle-stiff,
the given thanks, you've known
the lifted hook of every wave
can gaff you to the bone.

Nets on the rails, and walls of webs,
nets written on the wind;
I took the black book of the rock
as anchor for my mind.
I took the bent moon for my ring,
the big sail for my sheet,
but death strung nets out like a drift
across the climbing street.

The islands knocked their holes in tides;
the great cliffs locked their door.
I heard the clapper-trap of gulls
shout on the shell-bright shore.
But winter stiffened skies to wood
and nailed them on the eye.
I had four sons come home from sea
and only one was dry.

The fishbox houses crowd me round,
the windows black as rocks.
The gulls scream round the harbour sky;
the ropes scream through the blocks.
I wake up from the sleep of breath
and breath chokes breath like mist
within the crying of the gulls
that my three sons have kissed.

I walk in Virgin Street alone
through nets like cataract;
the watchers on the drystone steps
are dressed in fisher black.
I walk out by the iron pier
that straddles the used sand,
and tidals of the thigh and breast
turn on the lover's hand.

Roust out your prayers and mercies now
to tailor weeds for grief;
I split the word jammed in my jaws
with time's scaled gutting knife.
I lay my child-torn belly on
the friday of the stone;
the elder clasps his cockle hands
and all my grace is done.

Nets write their frenzied scribbles out
upon the gull-shrill air;
my one son looks out on the sea
and knows his muscles stir.
He turns his wrist upon the wood
as time turns in my side.
The shoaling cards fall like a wave
and spill his fortune wide.

Put back the cards; they slide like fish
and spell the same deep end.
I'd walk the eel-sleek shine of waters
to his reaching hand
but shuttles tear the netting fingers
and the cord is cut.
I touched the black book of the rock
and found my heart was wet.

My heart a sea, deep, green and black,
my fingers whitened shell,
my eyes blind as the blinded thing
that pulses the dumb pool,
and my wit cut, his oars rove through
the trammels of the sea.
I had four sons got by the tide
and tides have broken three.

I had four sons across my bed
below the weed-green wall;
under the hunting of the gulls
you'll hear their voices call,
and one and one and one again
they sweep across my eye,
blind hands held to the blinding sea
and my grey belly dry.

A BALLAD OF THE SEA

Pitch me down what way waves will,
the black green grows mast-high
and all the long sleep of the night
my wake streams out to die.
Whatever now or then I mind
the seam runs out like light
a nightspan from the climbing town
and all the fishes bite.

There's nights I ship more weight of wave
than clipper round the Horn
the gales of days Dad winked his eye
to have me kicking born,
and time whips through the fingers
and the stars are thick as sand
between Orion and the Cross
a midnight off the land.

The wake runs out. I wake to this
each darkness of the day.
You'll hear the blindness judged me
if you'll hear what sailors say.
But sailors talk in drifting words —
twilight's the time to catch.
I turn the corner of the sea
with every word I touch.

Past light and out. The women walk
the harbour and the slip.
I've had my five hooks in the gills
of many a lurking fish.
I've deep fished many a belly
and you'll know the catch in that,
but now no woman's broader armed
than her I'm steering at.

There's no tart keeps her darkness
close as the close sea,
and there's no bawdy madam
can block the door to me
or haggle cost. You pay all out
to ride the rocking bed
and learn the porpoise muscles leap
the deep's breached maidenhead.

You pay all out. The nets slide down
the fathomless I see,
for all is black as she was black
the hour she mastered me.
Whores take you far, but farther out
until your groin runs sand
every spermy penny's spent
into the deep fished sound.

I'd give my eyes again for nights
the blindness brings me back.
Pitch me down what way waves will,
I've learned the muscle's crack,
and now I'm all the wave she was
and death sinks like a lead
into the blackness I am grown
and gropes the dark sea bed.

Maybe it's talk. The talk comes out
like spittle on the tune
the ram-tam waves drum off the rocks
when rings burn round the moon.
Maybe it's all my blinded eye,
for words drift like a net
under the currents of the night
when the great sail is set.

And set it is. The wake streams out.
I hear the stillness come.
I ride the stillness as the storm.
The swinging buoys are dumb.
The caging buoys where men can claw
their wrecked souls from the sea
dip quiet as the lobster pots
on the green weed quay.

The quiet is. The whalebacked hills
lie over and at rest.
The bitch that pulled my breeches down
sleeps half across my chest
and will not wake, though my wake seams
the long night till the dawn
and all my silver money's spent
within the darkness' arms.

Now, then, I am. Put that word down.
Death stirs me like a tide.
The great grave lead swings down into
the fathoms of my side;
within the fathoms of my side
the soundings drop like lead,
and all the tidals of my breath
rock at the crossed masthead.

I tell you now the fishes run
the quiet of the sea
is stiller than the chapel stone
that one day covers me;
and still and dark the night tide runs
and each day till I fall
is darker than the darkness that
at first was over all,

the first creation and the last
to have its judgement rung.
By Bishop's Rock I've been as near
as most to Kingdom Come,
for Kingdom Come lifts like a wall
from the deep sound of the dead,
and the Northern Cross drops like a gannet
past the crossed masthead;

and I'll go down. I've had my slap
and tickle of the spray.
She sleeps her sweat out on my chest
and all the light's to pay.
But pitch me down what way waves will
I've nothing to regret.
The black green rocks the crossed masthead
and the great sail is set.

A BALLAD OF NEED

For John Knight

I nudge my black sleeve on the harbouring
brown bar of the pub.
O Angels properest to the diamond
emery of love's rub
that's cornered me upon the Word
and raps the running grain,
swing through the glass doors' darkness now
and clarify my name.

I am my need, and my need's that
the hungering gender shouts
locked in the cellar of the Book
to keep the bonelight out,
to keep the incandescent bone
dowsed and bushelled black
lest holy sex stand up and sing
Love Aphrodisiac.

Shame is a jacket on the bone
and sewn up to the chin
in case the sly unbuttoning light
might let love's finger in,
and prisoning palace, tower and stair
ignore birth's blood and straw,
but need grasps at necessity
and breeds in its own maw.

I'll not say No. Put back that book.
I'm bitter to defend
the hungering of my own racked flesh
until the world shall end.
I have my hungers common with
the commonest folk that bleed
beneath time's small incessant claws;
O Magnify my need.

Make need my Church. The niggling priest
tells Christ a moralist.
Break anger up into the throat;
they pander where he kissed.
They take man's fleshed and hungering God
who lived the needs we bear
and lug Him up to dogma's daughters
by a keyhole stair.

They dress the Anarch Avatar
like any mannequin
tricked out to show the nicest route
to fashionable sin —
the sin against the Ghost, the Ghost
that is the worm and fire.
O turn the priests into the street
and magnify desire.

Stand brothering here and fill your cup.
I speak because I know
the self-starvation of the tricked
and tricking puppet show
that acts out love like lawyer's cant
and ties Christ's bloody bands
on every deed of self abuse
conveyanced by priests' hands.

I speak because need burns my throat
to lift my pint to you
whoever you may be that walk
in pain and pity through
the swinging darkness of this door
that opens like a grave
to put your five bones next to mine
and share the time we have.

To you I drink. The nations fight
like children over bricks.
Possession is the power to give
what your own neighbour lacks.
And lack is your own neighbour's gift
to make time's meaning tall.
The lonely drinker and the thief
are crucified by all.

Need is my name. I stand here in
the hubbed and spinning world
that like a fury in the bud
lies intimately curled
to break its need out on the spring
and give the sun a name:
but heaven mocks the lovers' need
and burns it with need's chain.

I ask no heaven, Angels, none,
but clarify my need.
Make pride my humbling urgency
to heal the hands that bleed;
make want my gnawing wisdom that
I tell the bread from stone
and love no God but my own brother
latched within his bone.

One dispensation's all I ask
now as time is called.
Grant me no God that I may make
the want of man my world —
the want of man freed from a God
who's named but to betray —
that my own need may burn my flesh
and all my deaths away.

Here in the shouldering crowd of brothers
locked with want till time,
O Angels properest to the diamond
darkness of hearts' mine,
let me but break one vision free —
to be the love I need.
O Christ, O God, protect my wounds
and hymn them as they bleed.

A BALLAD OF BIRTH

For Sylvia

Shake me a handsome sunset down
while I am gay with wet.
The podded people in the church
are singing to forget
their God was belly-jumping once,
and shouldered out His cry
from flesh that swagged a nine-month long,
and danced a birth-creased thigh.

The pods split like the steepled fingers
of each childhood's joke.
The people wear their hoods of gaze
in case the light might look;
the people rivet knees and hands
in case their flesh might walk
and see in flesh their boneless God
whose four bones they broke.

I Am is the first bright thing,
and what is it comes next?
Shuffle your waters on my skull
and dig out your dead text.
Protect me from the world, the flesh,
the devil, and the truth:
you'll find my burning winter freeze
your monkeying wisdom tooth.

I'll upend all your days and ways
with my unfocused eye,
fiddle my fingers till your Rome's
black ashes mock the sky,
dance out my life until you dance
like strugglers on a string
to find the noose of your own love
a knot below the chin.

Look through your glass. The snow moves down
the leisurely of sky
until the brown earth's lathered white
and all the pools are dry,
shivered and shaken into fixed
white mirrors blank as stone.
The frost flares ash out on the branch
as my breath is begun.

Winter my wit, my knowledge all
the masterdom you see
alive in the twigged fingers fringed
on the bird-catching tree;
suds wink in sinks, sheets shake their sides,
time turns within its hide:
one winter night you'll die to know
what your own child has cried.

Turn me a river on the floor;
spill red suns from your back;
marble your meteors along
the nursery of time's track;
wall words with seas upended and
plant menhirs in the hall:
no house holds nevers big enough
to guard the word I call.

O you're a man and I a wink
once in your knocking eye,
but you'll have nevers guard your keys
till all the seas go dry:
you'll make your words, but I am Word,
though dumbening as I fall,
and carry this great shout of birth
through all the silenced world.

Chain me, chain the burning babe,
I'll not grow the less sure,
though time will double-lock my blaze
behind an ash-grey door,
and each grave politician blind
birth's comet eye with brass
and watch all generation through
the jawbone of his arse.

They starve all sinners from the flesh
and blood of sinner's meat,
and many a bishop carries guns
within his shovel hat,
and many a priest trains sights upon
the sparrow of His word:
shake me a handsome sunset down
before I break the world.

World breaks, world breaks as I down-leap,
analogy of end.
I latch my wrinkling hands on air,
locked in a swaddling band.
I cry a language newer than
the oldest truth of all.
Hold me your own and loneliness
and shield me lest I fall.

Guard me and ward; I need no guard,
but you need all of me,
the blaze of judgement petalled in
your own fleshed frailty;
the anarch and the avatar
whose hands and eyes you prayed
lies in the lying world of death
that your own lies have made,

lies in the cradling swing of seas,
the scooping seams of sky,
the hollowed clay, to learn your words
and look through your own eye.
Raise up your ghost's announcement of
the triumph that he brings:
Birth Is — Birth is the bright reply
and the whole winter sings.

A BALLAD OF THE WATCHER

For Percy Jarrett

Flick the match upon your nail
and have a smoker's drag;
whatever way the cat will jump
out of the gunny bag
there'll be a watcher of the game.
Time spins a threadbare yarn
but underneath the shouting flesh
there's silence in the bone.

We have the histories' account
and pay it on the nail;
the generations bleed their flowers
within an iron rail;
and voices lift and voices call;
the light and dark divide.
I cast my question at the word
and hear it tear my side.

Words words words are hammered down
until the planks are mad,
and words words words the woman shouts
in her hard-elbowed bed,
and words and words the gaunt cross lifts
its echo to the sky.
May there be one word at my head
when I lie down to die.

You'll get no language out of hock
by paying questions back;
for words that are the words that mean
you dig beneath the rock;
and daylight is a narrow chink,
a knife-slit in the door
that locks us down into the dark
of after and before.

I throw the bones down on the road
to turn my number up.
I throw them from the ignorant echo
of a painted cup.
It's not what is, but what will be
the way you let words fall.
I spit my sentence on the stone
and lean against the wall.

Who can become without he learn
he is himself alone,
or learn himself without he cut
his passion to the bone?
Who can walk armed into his peace
or naked face his war?
And who can get to his own bed
by his dead neighbour's door?

Who can walk the black-green sea
or thread the endless tide?
Who can take out the crying head
from his own bandaged side?
O who can find his own still face
that never lifts the glass,
or reach to love who has not loved
the difference of the race?

You have the blind man's mandolin
when coloured crowds go by;
you have the girls in liquid clothes
with roses at the thigh;
you have the black wall black with wet
beside the prison gate:
black as the penny and the pit,
Man stands on Ararat.

You'll see his face a step away.
The eyes are bald as stone.
From darkness we create the world
our ignorance has known,
and over there, a step away,
a prophet or a whore
waits for the terrible dead question
in the darkness door.

I let the historied greatness drop
and learn a simple thing;
there is no understanding more
than what the knife can sting;
and through the muscled leap and twitch,
the threads of ear and eye,
we pass to stand like Ararat
when time has ebbed us dry.

The clapping ghosts are crowding air.
The cities burn like blooms.
The white-hot rivets of the tears
sing in the inward rooms.
The father breaks his lover back
to heave time's girder free,
and palaces like wet salt crumble
into the lifting sea.

The trumpet of the child's long tear
will rubble bastions down;
the judgement of the lovers' bed
will sentence all we've grown;
the flicker of the Watcher's match
rasped on the black wet wall
will blaze its blindness out upon
and clarify us all.

A BALLAD OF FULFILMENT

I walk your own identity
this historied house we are.
Above the birdcrossed thatch of sky
there is a stable star
and in the black well under
the green wave of each sheet
a planet drowns; I walk in you
to watch those axes meet.

Speech is common to us all
and common words attend
the commonplaces we live in
until the dark descend;
the words worn smooth and dull and hard
grow simple as a stone
and simple is what addles me
when I lie down alone.

Simple is what dumbs my talk;
when syllables grow spare
what is there but the silent hand
and the togethered air?
I ask a way of telling
more than make the tale:
I scratch a dark word in the dust
with my hangman nail.

I am what is. The long watch spins
time's changing weathers round;
the dead past seams the dark like milk;
lamps lure the whale-backed land;
rock islands wart the skin-slick sea
that slides its muscles down
to reach a storm of mackerel up
into the stone-jawed town.

I launched my rib. The waters broke
black on the hagbacked rock
watching from out the whitehorsed waste
with death's old-fashioned look.
A woman in the place of nets
broke thread to see me pass
across the light, my solitude
cold as a looking glass.

My rib was launched. Slid like an eel,
my never, caulked with tar
to keep the temporal tidals out,
rocked out beyond the bar,
rocked out to write birds on the wind;
a thousand names were signed.
The black nets of the wind and weather
hauled them from my mind.

The lashed spray stung. The cords rasped harsh,
harsh as the redding lead
that shouts its dance of corks across
the fishscaled gutting shed,
and red was on the leaping silver,
red the eye of day;
the great drift of the wind and weather
dragged my speech away.

I ask you now, for now is all
the asking to be done,
what is the language of my track
below the scurrying sun?
What is the meaning of the meant
significance we guess?
Love's fisher hands were cross-tree nailed
and they were nailed to bless.

We fix a fisher face on love
and voyage our own flood;
the warp of every netting shuttle
grows from our own blood,
is rooted in our nesting bones
and leafed green with our tears
before its mesh upon the deep
the visage of our years.

We know the simple name I AM
and that is all we know.
But I AM is the thing we are
and all we overthrow
in naming it with words at all,
for I AM still is dumb
and, underneath the shouting flesh,
the hieroglyphic bone.

Bone's under all. I am what is.
I have a name for breath.
The woman in the place of nets
smiles with the smile of death.
I'd make the phrases big enough
if words would brace them tall,
but silence tides the marrow bone
and bone is under all.

Tides are the deafening quiet roared
within the marrow track.
I launched my rib upon the tide
to get my own death back.
Nine months my cargo chopped its ropes
round in the weltering sound;
my voyage of every mankind century
beached upon dead land.

I was a boy that had been racked
to fit love's narrow door.
There was no doubt that it was love:
the ten commandments wore
their great stone faces out to show
love meant the end of sin,
and sin began that hour that love
creaked wide to lock me in.

Love watched like flame my hedgerow days
laned down towards the sea
that called me from my father's word
engraved as history;
love broke my father's tomb in two
and dried my mother's womb.
I stole from where my mother sat
black in her netting room.

I asked the clouds my kind and kin
and had the wind reply.
I stole a clew from the nettled web,
a tear from the spider's eye;
I robbed the talk of the talking stones
of a penny word,
and thieved a sheet from the hanging line
to sew my sleep a shroud.

My father's ghost stared from the Church
and spoke a Book's reply.
I stole a thread from the beggar's sleeve
to sop my ponded eye.
I looked down at my father's Book
but found no answer yield
as under the crook-leg of love's star
I walked his flagstone field.

The hills like houses crowded round,
the windows black as rock;
the spider seines swung wet on briars;
the moon of bladders shook:
I picked a sin as gold as light
the everylair I turned
and in the swung scoop of the dark
I dreamed my body burned.

Guilty or not? I questioned all
the darkness and the light.
Feather and silk swing soft as milk
to make the big fish bite,
and in the green well of each dream
the light and dark divide:
I flicked my question at a hook,
choked on the word it cried.

Choked on the word. A woman lay
and watched me by the slip.
No dark was darker than her eyes,
red redder than her lip.
She lay there on the simple stone
and black nets shawled the light.
Feather and silk swing soft as milk
to have the leaper bite.

O whistle a wind or a woman
or sing a seal ashore;
a woman's half a mermaid
and the sea is half a whore:
my father's grave stood stiff as dust;
the grooved oar took my hand;
the black and white scream of the gulls
abandoned the dead land.

Black is black the red rust shouts
from the hangman chain,
and white is white the white steam roars
from the black-handled train;
O white is white, and black is black,
black as the flat black ray
that dragged its lash up from the deep
and slimed the white causeway.

I'm no philosopher to twist
the meaning of a need
that fumbles buttons in the dark
until the genders bleed,
but I'll tell one word red to stop
the traffic of the priest:
love was that Lord's discovery, and
He loved where love was least.

Love was that Lord's discovery, and
He found it in the pin
that linched the gallows tight to bear
the body he walked in.
He found it in the pin and web
of every crooked eye,
but we look through a cataract
to dream his crossed bones dry.

It takes a word to show a word
the hole within its head;
the dead-remembering dialect
shakes at the each thing said;
we stare through webs of our own bone
and hear the marrow tide
its great unsyllables within
the hooked and fisher side.

I launched my rib that lover tide
and heard bones voice the day.
I'd learn the dialect to tell
the agonies they say,
and wake my words till time is filled
for only then can He
present the silence I have learned
and let the bones go free.

I am what is. The long watch drives
the historied white wake back.
I search the language I am spoken
by time's voyaged track.
I find an angel lift a wave;
I know my brother sing
ascendant to the holy ghosts
of every living thing.

I tell you what you are I am.
The black nets drag our tide.
The simple words are bare as stone
to spell the clay we cried.
The simple words rock out to dark
and hear the graveward call,
but love lifts silence through the bone
and love is under all.

A SECOND BALLAD OF THE MUSE

Slip me the question of your need.
She walks the wakeful street
dressed up to undress your shaking
metric in her sheet.
O tart and sweet her high heels clack
the paved and asking stones
to shake her window-shopping ass
at every lust you own.

Oh yes, I know my words are coarse
as any groper's hand
locked in the doubling darkness with
a woman to be manned,
but what's the use of prettying up
the black cap of the law?
She walks the sensual street to die
the bought deaths of the whore.

O whore she is and tricked to kill.
The rustling shower coat
shines wetly as she swings her hips
along the stilt-heeled street.
Tricked out to kill, she'll die tonight
and any hour you pray.
O give your ghost a rendezvous
and muscle it away.

She is the fancy tart that knows
the fetish and the whip,
can fall each wrestler appetite
that burns you in its grip;
Goddess, child, queen, beast, and clown,
she has a greenroom thumb
to play out every act of breath,
but her last act is dumb.

Over behind the mammoth store
or by the boneyard wall
you'll find her leaning up against
the quiet of us all.
O call her on the telephone
and have a blinded date,
or meet her by the rain-black statue
and lose all you get.

Stand at the corner of time's street
and chance her sentence come.
As casual as an offered match
the huge disasters drum.
Imagination breaks your heart
while truth's paraded lies
high-heel their sweet sixteenings past
with down-lashed sidelong eyes.

O send her a letter scrawled with X.
Book the hotel room.
Time is the one she'll cheat you with
when you leave her alone.
Time is the stranger padding up
the rented winding stair
to find her listening for the key
with her white body bare.

O Time's the stranger smiling as
you squire her paid-up charms;
and Time's is that black scented glove
she lays upon your arm;
and Time's the fancy gentleman
that taught her how to please
and let your casual fingering linger
on her expensive knees.

Nylons rasp the furtive palm.
The shining belt unlocks.
There's meaning in the meantime mouth
that tongues her speaking looks.
The phrasing silks slip down her thighs.
The breasts of words elide.
This is the telling moment and
the told word breaks the bride.

Tickle her fancy if you can
or catch her on her day
and for the anything you give
she'll give herself away,
and easy is as easy does,
but, O, the cost is dear
when she stands in the coffin door
and asks the wage of fear.

Stood in the coffin doorway with
her high heels and her bag,
she lifts her black gloves to her lips
and takes a heavy drag;
she blows the smoke out on the night
that sailors tell her by,
and prophecies like black spent matches
ruin the wide sky.

O I've paid up and I've paid down
and found the bargain dear.
The body bared will burn you if
your lust wakes out of fear.
The naked flesh will scald your side,
the tongue destroy your tongue,
if you take thought of any cost
as her word is begun.

Expensive and expendable
as any appetite,
the bell-push nipples jut out hard,
the naked arms hold tight;
the syllabling of thighs cries out
till the great verb appals.
O body is how body dies
to answer that last call.

O body is when body dies
to have that word descend.
Strip in the syntax of her smile
and she'll spell out your end;
she'll burn her vision through her verb
until all meanings crack,
but Time is the lodger on the stair
and her last word is black.

POETRY FROM SONO NIS PRESS

JOHN BARTON
A Poor Photographer

MARILYN BOWERING
The Killing Room

ROBERT BRINGHURST
Bergschrund

JENI COUZYN
The Happiness Bird

JOHN ROBERT COLOMBO
Neo Poems

GWLADYS DOWNES
Out of the Violent Dark

RALPH GUSTAFSON
Gradations of Grandeur

THERESA KISHKAN
Ikons of the Hunt

LALA KOEHN
Forest Full of Rain

CHARLES LILLARD
Drunk on Wood
Voice, my Shaman

RONA MURRAY
Selected Poems
Journey

SUSAN MUSGRAVE
Selected Strawberries

HAROLD RHENISCH
Winter

JILL ROGERS
Alternate Endings

STEPHEN SCOBIE
The Rooms We Are

ROBIN SKELTON
Callsigns
Landmarks
Collected Shorter Poems 1947-1977

SEAN VIRGO
Pieces for the Old Earth Man
Deathwatch on the Skidegate Narrows

CHRISTOPHER WISEMAN
An Ocean of Whispers

DERK WYNAND
Snowscapes

J. MICHAEL YATES
Nothing Speaks for the Blue Moraines
Breath of the Snow Leopard
Fugue Brancusi

ANN YORK
In This House There Are No Lizards

ROBER ZEND
From Zero to One